my brother fights Pirates (well... kind of)

written by Missy Vaughn

illustrated by Earl Musick

design & layout by Jason Batt

This book is dedicated to Jody Vaughn.

An amazing husband and dad who with confidence said, "let's do this."
He is a true man.

Almost all families have a mom.

A lot of families have a dad.

Some have a brother or a sister.

And others have a ton

. . . like 2,000.

but only a few can say

they live with

Peter Pan.

Peter Pan loved adventures.

He had a big imagination

and he liked to fight pirates.

He really enjoyed being a kid.

That is just like my brother,

well, except for the pirate part.

My brother was born with Down syndrome.

He loves to play, laugh, hug

and, especially, make people smile just like other kids...

but sometimes he does things his own way.

Let me tell you about my brother...

Playing basketball is his favorite game.

He tries and tries

to get the ball in the hoop,

and with a little boost,

he can make the basket.

I love playing ball with him!

My brother loves to tell jokes!

"Knock knock."

I say, "Who's there?"

"Boo," he says.

I say, "Boo Who?"

He replies, "Please don't cry,
it's just a joke!"

He is really funny!

Most brothers like to camp.

So does mine...

And he becomes

the "wacky warrior wood boy"

that keeps our camp protected.

I feel safe.

And while other brothers are too cool for a hug...

Maybe even a little embarrassed,

That's not my brother...

he is always ready.

He gives the best hugs...
He makes me feel loved.

Sometimes my brother plays football with me,

and sometimes he is on the sidelines cheering me on!

Even though my brother can play football too,

he has lots of fun cheering everyone on

with his pots, pans and whistles!

He might not know it yet,

but I am his biggest fan!

We like to eat dinner together,

sometimes we make a mess.

Clean up is not our favorite thing,

but together we make a great clean up crew.

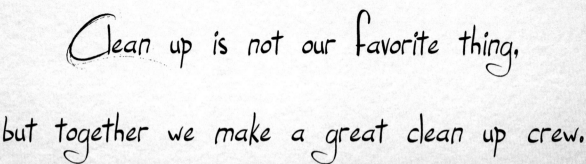

While many brothers run super fast,

my brother is easy to catch

. . . but hard to find.

He picks the best hiding places.

Some brothers have fish to feed.

So they feed the fish.

My brother tells them a story,

gives the tank a kiss

and feeds them one by one.

The fish really like my brother the best.

My brother has a great imagination.

I love when he turns into

CAPTAIN TOILET PAPER,

and saves the world,

one roll at a time.

Other brothers simply say "Good Night."

my brother does a silly dance

as he shouts

"Nighty night! night! night!"

and chases us with his toothpaste.

Sometimes I chase him back!

My brother is so much fun!

Most other brothers can talk,

they use their words.

My brother talks, but he can be hard

to understand sometimes...

so he uses his hands to sign to us.

That is pretty neat!

I love talking with my hands!

Many brothers go to school to learn.

My brother goes to school, too.

He also goes to speech therapy

to practice using his words,

and to physical therapy,

so he can catch us quicker

when we run.

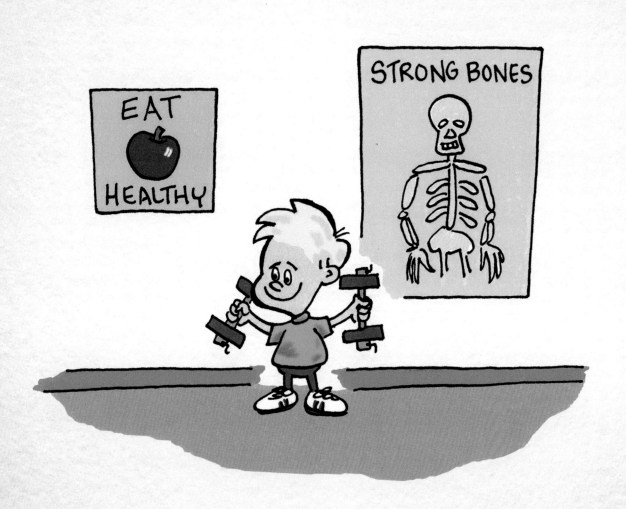

I hope he doesn't get too fast.

My brother and I love to climb trees together.

He fights the army of ants

about to take over the world

and he usually wins.

I'm glad he is on my side!

My family is pretty much like other families,

We love to laugh, eat, sleep

and play together...

The only big difference is that

My brother was born with Down syndrome.

He has helped us to see

that although we are not all the same...

we are more alike than different.

I love my brother!

My brother is fun.

My brother is loved.

My brother is smart.

Unlike Peter Pan, my brother will grow up.

I don't know what he will be when he gets big,

but I do know he will still be my brother.

I'll always enjoy the adventures

we have together along the way.

And while other brothers are great...

not many can say that

Peter Pan lives in their house.

And that is pretty cool.

And the fact that he fight pirates,

well okay, not really, but if he did...

I would be right by his side.

dedication

Dedication is not difficult when things are easy.
But when dedication exists in someone's life during a difficult situation, that is love.

We are dedicated to making Logan's life, our life,
our family's lives and anyone that will read this book
know that there is joy beyond belief with the words "Down syndrome."

A special thanks to the sisterhood for uniting together, becoming a supportive family
and paving the way for our kids one sister at a time

about the author

I am a wife and mother to four amazing children- Jada, Asher, Logan, and Davis. When planning for children, you think of the perfect world. You start to dream and imagine what they will look like and what they will become. From the color of their eyes and hair to their personalities...you imagine perfection. When our third child was born, what we had imagined as "perfect" was a little altered. When given the news that our son had Down syndrome, we were filled with so many questions and concerns. It didn't take long for us to realize that he was a perfect gift that God had entrusted to us. Through it all, we wouldn't change a thing.

When Logan's siblings asked what Down syndrome was, we had a hard time figuring out how to explain what this diagnosis might look like to them. Then it hit me- a great way to help kids understand Logan- he is like Peter Pan! I have always loved Peter Pan- he was adventurous, was a lot of fun to be around, and people were drawn to him. He enjoyed the little things in life, the things adults sometimes overlook. We see similar traits in Logan at this stage in his life. Our fun loving three year old has helped us to slow down and enjoy life to the fullest. Although we know he will grow up to be an amazing man, he will grow and mature in his own way and on his own timeline.

Our kids know that Logan is an amazing brother and that Down syndrome isn't a scary thing. I was inspired to write this book to help other children with a new brother or sister with Down syndrome. I also want to help other kids and parents feel comfortable knowing that although life with a family member with Down syndrome may be a different road to travel, it's an amazing journey to be on.

We thank God that we have Logan in our lives. I hope that *My Brother Fights Pirates (Well…Kind Of)* will be a great conversation starter for you and your family, opening the door to a broader discussion of the wonderful qualities that people with Down syndrome bring to a family.

Read more about our amazing adventure:

IHAVETHEGOLDTICKET.BLOGSPOT.COM

Made in the USA
San Bernardino, CA
21 March 2017